XTREME SPORTS

KITE SURFING

EPIC

BY RACHEL GRACK

EPIC, AN IMPRINT OF BELLWETHER MEDIA BY FLUTTERBEE

EPIC

EPIC BOOKS are no ordinary books. They burst with intense action, high-speed heroics, and shadows of the unknown. Are you ready for an Epic adventure?

This edition first published in 2027 by Bellwether Media, Inc.

For information regarding permission, write to Bellwether Media, Inc., Attention: Permissions Department, 3500 American Blvd W, Suite 150, Bloomington, MN 55431.

Library of Congress Cataloging-in-Publication Data is available at www.loc.gov or upon request from the publisher.

ISBN: 9798898800970 (hardcover)
ISBN: 9798898802219 (ebook)

Editor: Kieran Downs   Designer: Jeffrey Kollock

Printed in the United States of America, North Mankato, MN.

TABLE OF CONTENTS

WILD RIDE	4
WHAT IS KITESURFING?	6
THE HISTORY OF KITESURFING	10
KITESURFING TODAY	16
GLOSSARY	22
TO LEARN MORE	23
INDEX	24

WILD RIDE

A kitesurfer pops out of the water. She pulls the control bar and tips the kite to catch the wind. She zips across the water.

She jumps up and pulls the board into the air. What a ride!

HIGH SPEEDS

In 2017, a rider rode 67 miles (107 kilometers) per hour while kitesurfing. This was a world record.

WHAT IS KITESURFING?

Kitesurfing is an extreme water sport. Riders use boards and are pulled by special kites.

People can kitesurf on waves or smooth water. They need large spaces of open water.

FAMOUS LOCATION

OAHU

LOCATION	Hawaii, United States
FAMOUS FOR	Kitesurfing locations known for their scenic views

Kites and boards come in many shapes and sizes. The type of board depends on the rider's skill and riding style.

KITESURFING GEAR

Riders **steer** using a control bar and fly lines. They wear a **harness**, life vest, and other safety gear.

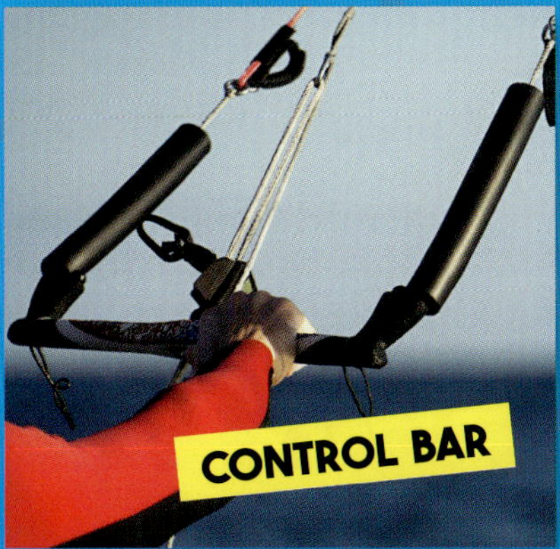

THE HISTORY OF KITESURFING

patent

In 1977, a **patent** was filed for a new water sport. It involved a board being pulled by a parachute.

Two French brothers worked on the idea. In 1984, they invented a kite that floats in water.

FLOATING KITE

In 1994, KiteSki was released. This system used a kite and water skis. Later, the skis changed to a board.

In 1996, Laird Hamilton showed off kitesurfing in Hawaii. It helped the sport grow!

LAIRD HAMILTON, 1996

KITESURFING IN MAUI, HAWAII

FAMOUS FACE

GISELA PULIDO

BIRTHDAY	January 14, 1994
HOMETOWN	Premià de Mar, Spain
FAMOUS FOR	Youngest kitesurfing world champion at age 10

TIMELINE

1977 A patent is filed for a parachute water sport

1984 Two French brothers invent a kite that floats

1994 KiteSki is released

1998 The first World Kitesurfing Championship takes place in Maui, Hawaii

2024 Kitesurfing becomes an Olympic event

In 1997, riders began using different types of boards. This helped the sport grow. The first World Kitesurfing **Championship** was held in Maui, Hawaii, in 1998.

In 2024, kitesurfing was added as an event at the Paris **Summer Olympics**.

KITESURFING EVENT AT THE 2024 PARIS SUMMER OLYMPICS

KITESURFING TODAY

Kitesurfing events are split into **disciplines**. Riders do tricks mostly on flat water in **freestyle** competitions.

A LONG RIDE

In 2015, a rider broke the record for longest nonstop kitesurfing ride. Francisco Lufinha rode for more than 47 hours straight.

Big air events see riders flying through the air in high winds.

big air

In kitesurfing races, riders speed through courses. **Hydrofoil boards** help riders go even faster.

Riders show off their kitesurfing skills on ocean waves in wave events.

HOW TO

KITE JUMP

1. Build speed
2. Move kite straight overhead
3. Pull bar into body
4. Push down on back foot and pull up front knee
5. Push bar away from body
6. Land with body over the board

A LOT OF AIR

The record for the highest jump while kitesurfing is 131 feet (40 meters).

RED BULL KING OF THE AIR EVENT

Red Bull King of the Air is an event that judges the best big air moves. Riders showcase sky-high jumps and tricks.

Riders keep finding new ways to have fast fun on the water.

GLOSSARY

big air—related to a style of kitesurfing where riders perform high jumps

championship—a contest to decide the best person or team

disciplines—certain styles of kitesurfing

freestyle—related to events based on tricks rather than time

harness—a special belt with straps that people can hook a rope into

hydrofoil boards—kitesurfing boards with tall fins that lift them out of the water

patent—a document that gives an inventor the right to be the only one to make or sell their invention for a certain number of years

steer—to control the direction of movement

Summer Olympics—a worldwide summer sports contest held in a different country every four years

TO LEARN MORE

AT THE LIBRARY

Grack, Rachel. *Snowboarding*. Minneapolis, Minn.: Bellwether Media, 2027.

Mazzarella, Kerri. *Kitesurfing*. New York, N.Y.: Crabtree Publishing, 2026.

Vonder Brink, Tracy. *Surfing*. Minneapolis, Minn.: Jump!, 2025.

ON THE WEB

FACTSURFER

Factsurfer.com gives you a safe, fun way to find more information.

1. Go to www.factsurfer.com.
2. Enter "kitesurfing" into the search box and click 🔍.
3. Select your book cover to see a list of related content.

INDEX

big air, 17, 20
control bar, 4, 9
freestyle, 16
gear, 8–9
Hamilton, Laird, 12
harness, 9
kite jump, 19
KiteSki, 12
Oahu, Hawaii, 7
Pulido, Gisela, 13
races, 18
Red Bull King of the Air, 20
Summer Olympics, 15
timeline, 14
World Kitesurfing Championship, 15

The images in this book are reproduced through the courtesy of: ohrim, front cover, pp. 1, 4, 5, 21; Wallenrock, front cover, pp. 1, 8; Ines Porada, front cover, p. 1; Ashraf Hamdan, front cover, pp. 1, 16; Vladislav Gajic, p. 2; Artur Didyk, p. 3; AlexAC21/ Wikimedia Commons, p. 5 (fun fact); EpicStockMedia, p. 6; susanne2688, p. 7 (left); Kyo46, p. 7 (right); CatwalkPhotos, p. 8 (inset); K-FK, pp. 8 (kite), 18 (inset); Oleg, pp. 8 (board), 21 (inset); Yankovsky88, p. 9; pavel1964, p. 9 (control bar); Vallehr, p. 9 (harness); KarepaStock, p. 9 (life vest); Pmau/ Wikimedia Commons, p. 10; US patent 4708078/ Wikimedia Commons, p. 10 (inset); JHVEPhoto, p. 11; Regular Daddy/ Wikimedia Commons, p. 11 (inset); Chuck Mason/ Alamy Stock Photo, p. 12; Bob Bekian/ Wikimedia Commons, p. 12 (inset); ZUMA Press, Inc./ Alamy Stock Photo, p. 13 (left); Hoch Zwei/ Getty Images, p. 13 (right); DPPI Media/ Alamy Stock Photo, p. 13 (bottom); Phil Walter/ Getty Images, p. 14 (2024); Lloyd Images/ Getty Images, p. 15; HENNING BAGGER/ Getty Images, p. 17; Associação +Mar/ Wikimedia Commons, p. 17 (fun fact); Villegas Photo, p. 18; Anadolu/ Getty Images, p. 20.